YOUR KNOWLEDGE HAS VALUE

- We will publish your bachelor's and
  master's thesis, essays and papers

- Your own eBook and book -
  sold worldwide in all relevant shops

- Earn money with each sale

Upload your text at www.GRIN.com
and publish for free

Bibliographic information published by the German National Library:

The German National Library lists this publication in the National Bibliography; detailed bibliographic data are available on the Internet at http://dnb.dnb.de .

Imprint:

Copyright © 2015 GRIN Verlag, Open Publishing GmbH
Print and binding: Books on Demand GmbH, Norderstedt Germany
ISBN: 9783668344303

This book at GRIN:

http://www.grin.com/en/e-book/343777/a-critical-review-of-sotunsa-s-features-of-talking-drum-poetry

Luqman Kiaribee

A Critical Review of Sotunsa's "Features of Talking Drum Poetry"

GRIN Publishing

GRIN - Your knowledge has value

Since its foundation in 1998, GRIN has specialized in publishing academic texts by students, college teachers and other academics as e-book and printed book. The website www.grin.com is an ideal platform for presenting term papers, final papers, scientific essays, dissertations and specialist books.

Visit us on the internet:

http://www.grin.com/

http://www.facebook.com/grincom

http://www.twitter.com/grin_com

Contents

Abstract

This paper is critically reviews Sotunsa's (2005), *"Features of Talking Drum Poetry,"* a doctoral thesis submitted to English Department, Faculty of Arts, University of Ibadan. To present this paper in a simpler form attempt has been made to divide it into sections. Section one discusses introduction which is the background to the paper, while section two (the abstract) discusses the paper's goals. The third section covers the summary of the thesis. Section four as well is a critical review of affirmations made by the author. We considered some scholars' views on these affirmations and looked at their genuineness. We made assumptions to rectify some views likewise we made comment to credit the genuineness of author's arguments where it is necessary. In the last section, we do the summary and make some recommendations in support of author's arguments established in the last chapter of the thesis. Our goal, in this paper, is to do a constructive criticism on Sotunsa's doctoral thesis basically, it is for academic purposes.

Introduction

> Yoruba oral poetry is a living and dynamic verbal art. It
> is meant to be sung, chanted, intoned in performance in
> the presence of an audience at a given social, religious,
> cultural, political or informal occasion. Its performance
> is usually accompanied with drum, music and dance...
>
> (Ọlajubu, 1981: 21, alluded by Sotunsa, 2005)

As stated in the above excerpts, the aesthetic of oral poetry cannot be over
emphasised. It is a tradition which cannot be neglected whenever general discussions
are being made on Yoruba literature. Evidence from literatures have shown that
Ọlatunji (1984), Finnegan (1970), Abimbọla (1968 and 1969) Babalọla (1966),
Ọlajubu (1982), Ọlabọde (1981), Ọbasa (1921), Olukoju (1994), Yemitan (1963 and
1970) among others have really discussed the features, structures and importance of
Yoruba oral literature. Despite the fact that scholars have worked and are still working
on non-verbal aspect of oral poetry (i.e. drum), the aesthetic of it still stands out. It is
on this note that this paper chooses to review the work of Sotunsa Mobolanle who
worked on *Features Of Talking Drum Poetry* so as to explore and unfold some
aesthetics of drum poetry discussed by the scholar. Also to comment critically on the
findings of the author.

3

The Summary of the Thesis

Before the detail of the thesis it is very much important to give the summary of its abstract. The thesis discusses the stylistic features and functional significance of drum poetry. This is shown by the author's statement made in the abstract.

The study reveals that talking drum poetry, like its oral counterpart requires a special skill and it is realisable only on actual performance. Although it shares many features with vocal form of poetry, it possesses its own unique stylistic attributes and aesthetic functionality.

p. vii –
viii.

This statement reveals that the author examines the talking drum as a unique poetic mode of its own which requires a special analysis like other oral poetry being a speech, a chant and a song mode. To establish her arguments, the author discusses her findings under six chapters;

In the first chapter, the author states the discussion base on argument whether traditional oral poetry should be considered poetry. To support her claims, the author quotes different scholars who are in support of the claim that traditional oral poetry is truly poetry on its own. Among the scholars she cites include Aderemi Bamikunle (1985:48), Ọlajubu (1981: 71), Emovon (1981: 205) and Finnegan (1992: 26). She further gives explanations on the features of traditional poetry which include the impact of performance art, the audience, the use of musical instruments and the theme of traditional African poetry. She gives evidence from different notable scholars like Wole Soyinka, Niyi Osundare, Kofi Awoonor, Chinua Achebe and others. Also in this chapter, the author discusses the place of the talking drum in Indigenous African oral poetry. Under this sub topic, the author reveals the scholars' views on the status of talking drum in African poetry. For example, she discusses Olukoju (1978: 83) which considered drum poetry as an aspect of speech mode of oral poetry. She proceeds by reviewing the view of Opefeyitimi (1995: 156) which considered the role of drum poetry as a lieutenant in Yoruba Orature Performance (YOP). The Nketia (1967), Akin Euba (1990) and different scholars view on the drum poetry were also reviewed. The author at this point makes a stand that the drum poetry role in oral poetry is beyond an auxiliary or lieutenant for the fact that it has its own unique features which

4

made it stand as a separate mode of an oral poetry like speech, chant and song mode. Lastly, in this chapter, the author explains her theoretical framework and the reason why she chooses to use semiological approach, functionalism, ethno-musicology and models/theories of communication.

In chapter two, the author continues reviewing the previous related works to her study. She looks into the work of various scholars like Adetoyese Laoye (1959) Echezona (1963), Euba (1960), Adegbite (1994), Ajayi (1987), Esinlokun (1997) among others on the nature, forms, functions and importance of drum poetry.

In chapter three, the author discusses the style in Yoruba drum poetry. Under this sub topic, the author makes a clarification by saying that drum poetry is membronic verbal communication and should be treated as such.

> It is verbal communication in the sense that the poetry
> can be analyzed linguistically. In addition it possesses
> its own unique style and can be differentiated from
> other forms of poetry, vocal or written. (p. 72)

Among the styles and aesthetics which the author recognises are the rhythmic and the intonation patterning of sounds, the musical nature of the poetry, the variation in pitch, the pauses, the vowel clustering, the gliding, the rhythmic elongation and the ambiguity nature of the poetry.

> The variation in pitch, pauses, and vowel clustering and
> gliding as well as rhythmic elongation, distinguishes
> drum speech from actual speech and endows it with a
> unique style of its own (p. 77)

To actualise her findings, the author makes use of computerized graphs to show the frequency of soundwave length of some selected texts. Two examples from these texts are:

1. 1. Ọmọ ẹkùn náà dà   Where is the leopard's offspring
       Ọmọ ẹkùn náà rè é   This is the leopard's offspring
    2. A-jí-ṣe bí - Òyó là á rí   We only see those who endeavour to
                                      imitate
       Òyó kìí ṣe bí baba ẹnìkankan   Òyó people are not imitators of
                                      anybody (p. 77)

5

At the end of this text, the author observes that there are more evidence of overtones, rhythmic elongation, variation in pitch, pauses, vowel clustering in drum versions of the tested texts compared to their voiced versions. Three criteria used by the author in the test include the pitch[1], the timbre[2] and the loudness[3] of the tone. Having explained these unique features, the author discloses;

> Drum poetry by virtue of its distinct style should earn
> recognition as a unique form of poetry by critics of
> indigenous literature, oral literature in particular.

(p. 99)

Chapter four comprises the application of the theoretical framework and theories explained in chapter two. The chapter, also, is the continuation of the style in Yoruba poetry, started in chapter three. The author here applies the literary and semiotic approach to analyse some Yoruba drum poetry. The data analysed are performances of drum poetry at different places among of which are;

i.   a performance of dundun drum set at the palace of Ọba Adetoyese Oyeniyi Odugbemi, the Olufi of Gbọ̀ngán in which the palace drummers rendered the praise poetry (oríkì) of the kind.

ii. also, the drum performance at the funeral party of Adigun Adele Làísì at Gbọ̀ngán town, Ọ̀ṣun State which was led by Mustafa Ayanniyi Ayanbode.

The author in these two samples transcribes the drum poetry into verbal, she gives the English translation and also does the critical analysis using semiological approach to assign meaning.

Before she rounds off this chapter, the author observes that the drum poetries for deities are mostly have fixed rhythms associated with concerned deity. One of the prominent examples used by the author is the Ogun drum performance (ìlú ògún) which was performed by one of her informants, Mr Jimoh Alayande.

2.1   Ogun gba 'já   Ogun please receive the dog

      Gba 'já   Receive the dog

      Sán san gidi   San san gidi

---

[1] Pitch: a term use in music which set a part or note into a particular musical scale
[2] Timbre: also called "tone colour", this is a property of sounds that distinguish it from other sound of the same pitch and volume.
[3] Loudness: This refers to the volume or amplitude of sound.

6

Sangidi	Sangidi
Ọdẹ jẹun tán	The hunter eats
Ọdẹ yó	The hunter is filled
Ọdẹ ṣekùn rogodo	The hunter's stomach becomes rounded
Ògún gb'ajá	Ogun please receive the dog
Gb'ajá	Receive the dog (p. 160)

Modern trends in Yoruba drum poetry is what the author discusses in the fifth chapter. The author here looks at the impact of drum poetry in contemporary popular music by saying that;

> It is not surprising; therefore, that Yoruba drum poetry
> is easily integrated into popular music, as they are twin
> arts, (p. 174).

The author continues by giving examples of popular Yoruba musicians who have successfully used the drum poetry in their music albums. Musicians like Roy Chicago, Adeolu Akinsanya, Bobby Benson, Dele Ojo, Sunny Ade, Ebenezer Obey, Dele Abiodun, Shina Peter were mentioned as successful musicians who have used drum poetry to create aesthetic in the music. That popular Sunny Ade's track "The Merciful God" in which the musician used drum poetry to render the track before singing it verbally was cited.

3. Mò ń yan fanda fanda
    Lójú apògàn
    Bí òpólò ṣe ń yan lójú ẹlẹgùsí
    Tẹlẹgúsí ò gbọdọ yí láta
    The merciful God (p. 189)

She also expatiates on the use of drum poetry in film industry (Theatre). She looks at the works of Ọla Rotimi (*Kúrunmí* and *The gods are not to blame*) and Akinwumi Iṣòla's *Ṣaworoidẹ* where the drum was used to checkmate the excessive rule of the tyrannical leader (Làgàta). Example of drum poetry which the author references in *Ṣaworoidẹ* is:

7

4. Aṣọ funfun ní sunkún aró	White cloth longs for indigo dye first
Ìpìlẹ̀ ọ̀rọ̀ ní sunkún èkejì tantantan	The first part of statement cried
	for the second
Adíá fún Adérọ́mọ́pò	We divined for Adérọ́mọ̀pò
Àjànàkú	The Elephant
Ọmọ Òní	Child of Òní
Ojọ́ tí mẹ́kún ń ṣe'ráhùn	The day a crying person agonizes
Ire gbogbo	All goodness
Tètè wá Jogbo wá o	Come quickly to visit Jogbo
Ire gbogbo	All goodness (p. 204 -5)

The use of drum poetry in the mass media is also discussed. She gives example of jingles which were composed in drum poetry to advertise, announce, sensitise and advise the populace by the mass media. One of such examples is the one used by Broadcasting Corporation of Oyo State to announce the commencement of their news.

5.	Bó ba ti rí ni ẹ wí	Say it just as it is
	Bó bá ti rí ni ẹ wí	Say it just as it is
	Àlá kìí bọmọ lẹ́rù	A dream is never too dreadful
	Kó má le è rọ	That a child cannot narrate it
	Bó bá ti rí ni ẹ wí	Say it just as it is (p. 210)

The last chapter (chapter six) discusses conclusion and recommendation of the work. In this chapter, the author concludes by making some recommendations on the use of drum poetry. Her suggestions and recommendations include the use of drum poetry as an instrument of mass mobilization, public enlightenment on various issues like supporting and participating in electoral processes, census, health-care, Child Survival and Development (CSD) etc. She also says that the information on the programme of the WHO, UNESCO, UN and some other world organizations can be spread to the grassroots through the use of drum poetry. Another recommendation she makes is that the drum poetry can be made an institute which people from other culture in any part of the world can visit as tourism.

In conclusion, the author on the last page of chapter six rounds off her explanation by saying:

Yoruba drum poetry is a unique cultural asset, which must be further explored, harnessed and exploited for the advancement of African cultures and indigenous technology.

The Critical Analysis of Findings and Affirmations in Sotunsa (2005); Features of Talking Drum Poetry

Doctoral thesis as shown by Hart (1998: 20 – 25) must fulfill seven requirements which the author claims to be generally agreed upon across the academic fields. These include, specialization in scholarship, making a new contribution to an area of knowledge, demonstrating a high level of scholarship, demonstrating originality, the ability to write a coherent volume or intellectual work, ability to develop the capacity and personal character to intellectually manage the research, including the writing of the thesis, and the showing of an in-depth understanding of the topic areas and works related to the research.

In her attempt to fulfill the requirements mentioned above, the author demonstrates high level of scholarship that made her come out with findings which we want to draw out and criticize later in this work.

i. Firstly, the author while agitating in support of the consideration of African oral poetry as poetry on its own opines:

> The text alone cannot constitute the oral poem. For this
> reason, no discussion of oral poetry can afford to
> concentrate on the text alone, but must take account of
> the audience, the context of performance, the
> personality of poet-performer and the details of
> performance itself (p. 4).

This excerpt shows that the author is in support of scholars like Olajubu (1981:71), Bamikunle (1985: 48), Emovon (1981), Finnegan (1992) who are all in support of the consideration of oral literature as an independent form of literature which its content and context goes beyond the text. For this reason, she is supposed to be kudos because this claim is true. Oral poetry is a distinct form of poetry and it must be treated as such.

ii. Credit should also be given to the author by modifying the stand of Opefeyitimi (1995: 156) which regards the function of talking drum as a lieutenant. The author said and I quote:

> While talking drummers do serve as lieutenants in some orature performance, it is also a fact that in other performances such as court salutation, the talking drummer is the main artist who may be accompanied by other ensemble players and singers as well as dancers (pp. 15 – 16)

To support this claim, a reference can be taken to music albums of Ayanyemi Atokowágbowónílé who's talking drum (dùndún) plays a role of lead singer which the chorus translates into verbal form.

iii. While reviewing the work of Ajayi (1987: 44) who referenced Faleti's claim on drum poetry as a genre that generates ambiguity, the author supports by saying that the drum poetry is ambiguous and it must be treated as such. The author moves further to recommend the act of familiarity with Yoruba idioms and wise-sayings, account of the contextual factors, knowledge of Yoruba tone system as a tool of understanding the drum poetry. The author emphases that, as said by Faleti in Ọlatunji (1982: 143), it is only the drummer that understands the poem poetry mostly;

Ṣùgbọ́n kò sẹ́ni tó mèdè àyàn	But no one understands the language of ‘
	Drummer
Bí ẹni t'ómọ́pàá ẹ̀ lọ́wọ́	Like the person who owns the stick
Ẹni tó gbómọle lọ́wọ́	It is he who is beating the drum
Ló mọ'un t'ómele ńsọ	That know actually what the drum is saying

With this observation and explanation, the author requires an accolade because the explanation shows her as a demonstrator of high level of scholarship.

iv. Another thing that distinguishes the work is the definition the author gives to talking drum. To most people (especially non-literary people), it is only dùndún drum set they regard as a talking drum of Yoruba musical instruments. This assumption is wrong because mostly all Yoruba drums can talk, these include agogo, aro, àjà, ṣẹkẹrẹ, igbá among others. She defines talking drum thus:

> …the talking drum is any musical instrument bearing the name 'drum' for example a membranophone[4] or a slit drum used as a speech surrogate (p. 68 – 69).

v.   We also agree with the author on the opinion that drum poetry is a membrionic verbal communication and it performs almost the same function the verbal version performs. Also, we agree with the author's claim that drum poetry unlike its verbal version can be linguistically analysed.

> It is a verbal communication in the sense that the poetry can be analysed linguistically. In addition, it possesses its own unique style, and can be differentiated from other forms of poetry, vocal or written (p. 72)

vi.   We submits to the author's opinion which recognizes the rhythmic and intonation patterning of sound, musicality nature, gliding of vowels, variation in pitch, pauses and vowel clustering, rhythmic elongation, repetition of lines, overtone, vibrating echoes, dancing and gesticulations as the aesthetic qualities of a talking drum.

> The variation in pitch, pauses and vowel clustering and gliding as well as rhythmic elongation, distinguishes drum speech from actual speech and endows it with a unique style of its own (p. 77).

vii.   We cannot close our eyes to the data collected by the author which include the dùndún performance at the palace of Ọba Adétóyèṣe Oyeniyi Òdúgbèmí, the Olúfì of Gbọ̀ngán in which the praise poetry of the king was rendered. Also the funeral poetry performance led by Mustapha Àyánníyì Ayanbọ̀dé at the funeral ceremony of Àdìgún Àdèlé Làísì at Gbọ̀ngán town, the drum performance poetry staged by Ìfẹ́lódùn Group of Drummers, under the directory of Mr Jimoh Alayande at Apòmù and the Ọbàtálá drum poetry performance by the same group but which was led by Mr Lasisi Ayande, Balógun Onílù of Apòmù, at Apòmù are among of the data anlaysed by the author.

---

[4] Membranophone: Any musical instrument that produces sound via the vibration of a stretched membrane.

11

Our observation is that the data depict the originality nature of drum poetry and it helps the author in doing a perfect analysis on the subject matter.

viii.   The author in her explanation on the relevance of drum poetry in contemporary popular music and theatre gives different example of excerpts and does a perfect analysis on drum poetries used by these artistes ranging from Sunny Ade, Adéolú Akínsànyà, Bobby Benson, Délé Òjó Roy Chicago to literary scholars like Ọla Rotimi, Wọle Soyinka, Chinua Achebe, Ọṣọfisan, Akinwumi Iṣọla and others who have successfully used drum poetry to create aesthetics in their works of art. This part shows an analytical and pragmatic analysis which is expected in a doctoral of philosophy thesis.

ix.   The author in her recommendation gives several suggestions through which the art of drum poetry can be sustained and retained for future generation. She also suggests ways through which the art can be globalised and be made a tourism business. To a greater extent, we agreed with the author and we suggest that if drumming art is put in extra curriculum activities of the primary and secondary school education, like how Brazil inculcates the habit of footballing into her young population right from childhood, the art of drumming will encounter a great and a quick development.

x.   Finally, we support the author in her counter argument against the categorization of oral poetry reviewed in Ọlatunji (1984). Contrary to the scholars reviewed, Ọlatunji (1984) recognises the feature type, the chanting and the song mode as types of Yoruba oral poetry. To rectify this, the author adds the drum mode, as an independent oral poetry which has its own peculiarity like others. She also redefines oral poetry as

> … a poetry whose distribution, composition and performance are essentially by word of mouth or through instrumental medium, which transmit aural decodable in human language (p. 214)

We agree with the author on thesis, but we disagree with her on some issues.

i.   We disagree with the author for supporting Ọba Laoye (1966:36) who listed "Bàtá" and "Bẹ̀nbẹ́" among the drum that are used for secular function without clarifying the fact that these drums perform dual function. Even there are anomalies in the functions of Àpèsí, Kùnbẹ́ or Gbẹ̀m-gbẹ̀m, Òkìrì and Ṣákárà which the author gives. The primary function of "Àpèsì" is ritual or religious while its secondary

12

function is the secular function which the author only made mention. As for Bàtá, it is associated with Ṣàngó religion (Daramọla and Jẹjẹ 1967: 171) while Àpèsì is the drum use in Orò cult. There are different forms of Bẹ̀nbẹ́, some Bẹ̀nbẹ́ are basically for ritual, they are called Bẹ̀nbẹ́ Òrìṣà, some are used in traditional marriage while some types of Bẹ̀nbẹ́ are associated with Islamic religion (Bẹ̀nbẹ́ Àsàlátù). This type of clarification is what we expect from the author.

The author also in page 54 supports Ẹsinlokun (1997: 10 – 17) which categorized Bẹ̀nbẹ́ under a ritual drum. This is an inconsistency of view on the part of the author. This is very misleading; the clarification as we said above supposed to be made so as to explain the issues that arise from categorization of Yoruba drum and the criteria used for such categorization.

ii.   Another area where we disagree with the author is her explanation on the way and method of playing Yoruba talking drum on page 36. On page 36, the author does not oppose Ademola Adegbite (1994: 52) which identified only two ways of playing talking drum. The first style which Adegbite identifies is the use of armpit to hold the drum and using underarm to press and release the drum to get the required tones. The second style is the use of thigh/hip to control the drum. In this control technique, the drum is held over the drummer's shoulder with a leather strap. So, the drummer uses the underarm to press the drum to the thigh/hip while the drum releases sound. We critically look into this explanation and we discovered that the styles account only for "dùndún" drum type (Ìyá ìlù, omele dùndún, kẹríkẹrì, àdàmọ̀, kànnàgó etc.). The techniques mentioned do not accounts for other talking drum like bàtá, ṣákárà, fèrè, àpèsì, igbìn, ṣẹ̀kẹ̀rẹ̀ and gúdúgúdú, supposed we go by the definition given to talking drum in page 68 – 69.

> … the talking drum is any musical instrument bearing
> the name 'drum' for example a membranophone or a
> slit drum used as a speech surrogate (pp. 68 – 69).

iii.   In chapter four and five of the thesis, data of different drum poetry were given which the author analyses using the semiotic, structuralism and some communication theories. Our observation about these data is; the author does not give us the direct

13

transliteration[5] of the data in tonal pattern before converting them into orthographic version as done by Fálétí in *Oníbodè Lálúpọn* where Fálétí transliterates the drum tone before given the orthographic version.

Tonal transliteration: Dan dan dan dàn dàn dàn

Dan dan dan dàn dán

Dan dan dan dan dán-án

Dan dàn dán dán dan

Verbal and Orthographic version:

Ẹ wẹnu ìmọ̀dò, ẹ wẹnu ìsín

Ẹ wẹnu Oníbodè Lálúpọn

or

Mo jẹun Èjìgbò, mo jẹun Ìwó

Mo jẹun Oníbodè Lálúpọn

The importance of this is that it helps the reader to relate the transliteration to the verbal and written form of the drum poetry data.

iv.   We have praised the author for recognizing the ambiguity nature of the talking drum, also for referencing Ajayi (1987: 44) who reviewed Adébáyọ̀ Fálétí's poem "Oníbodè Lálúpọn", but the author herself failed to give us examples of data in which drum poetry generates ambiguity. Whereas, there are a lot of examples which the author can cite even in the media industries she explored. There is a popular example in Radio Nigeria's Ibadan jingle which people interpret to different meaning:

Dín dìn dìn dìndíndín

Din dín dín dí din dìn

This is Nigeria Broadcasting Station

Among of the meaning which people ascribe to this are:

1.	Ó jọgẹ̀dẹ̀ dúdú	He eats unripe plantain
	Inú ń ta bọ̀n-ùn	His stomach protrudes
2.	Kò sónígbèsè níbí	There is no debtor here

---

[5] Transliteration: The act or product of transliterating or of representing letters or words in the characters of another alphabet or script.

14

Lọ sílé kejì	Go to the next house

3. BÓlúbàdàn bá kú   If Olúbàdàn dies

     Ta ni ó joyè   Who will replace him (etc)

These are the kind of examples we expect the author to deeply explain as regards the ambiguity nature of drum poetry.

v.   Lastly, the author in the abstract makes a suggestion on the need to break the traditional barriers of making the art of drumming a family profession.

> The study therefore suggests the need to break the traditional barriers of making the art a family profession in order to enable whoever is interested in the acquisition of the skill of drum poetry to do so. (p. vii – viii).

Our interview with Mr Dipo Johnson (a sax player) who is a postgraduate student of the University of Ibadan shows that music industries has gone beyond the tradition of making a drum art a family affairs/profession only. He said a lot of professional and independent drum players have emerged in music industry. He said some developed the skill independently, and some of them passed through formal music school. Also, Miss Ìbùkún who plays gángan at Redeem Christian Postgraduate Fellowship, Awo Park, University of Ibadan, explains that she does not come from traditional drum family but she develops the skill in her church in Lagos when she was around twelve years of age and since then she has been trying to improve herself before she became skillful. So the jinx of restricting the art to the family profession only is broken; and drum nowadays has become what people play perfectly irrespective of age, sex, race and tribe.

Conclusion

As we said earlier, our mission in this work is not to castigate or do a blind criticism on Sotunsa's doctoral thesis. We are very sure that our analysis in this review has proved that no one is an island of knowledge. The scholarship work goes beyond what a single person can be just to because as time changes, cultures, arts, behaviours, beliefs and thoughts complies with it. So, the genuineness of a scholarship thesis remains in the rebranding, reviewing and restating of some outdated

15

findings. So, there is a need for research students to keep on reviewing the outstanding research works so as to update the outdated affirmatives therein.

References

Abímbọ́lá, W. (1968), *Ìjìnlẹ̀ Ohùn Ẹnu Ifá: Apá kìíní.* Glasgow: Collins.

Abímbọ́lá, W. (1969), *Ìjìnlẹ̀ Ohùn Ẹnu Ifá: Apá kejì.* Glasgow: Collins.

Babalọla, A. (1966) *The Content and Forms of Yoruba Ijala.* Oxford: Clarendon Press.

Daramola, O. and Jẹjẹ, A. (1967), *Awọn Àṣà àti Òrìṣà Ilẹ̀ Yorùbá.* Ibadan: Oníbọn-òjé Press.

Finnegan, R. (1970), *Oral Literature in Africa.* Oxford: Nairobi.

Hart Chris (1998), *Doing a Literature Review.* London: SAGE Publication Limited.

Ọbasa, D.A. (1971), *Àwọn Akéwì Apá kìíní.* Ibadan: Oxford University Press.

Ọlabọde, A. (1981), The Semantic Basis of Metaphors and Related Tropes in Yoruba. Ph.D Thesis, University of Ibadan.

Ọlajubu, O. (1972) *Àkójọ Iwì Egúngún.* Lagos: Longman.

Ọlajubu, O. (1982) *Àkójọ Iwì Egúngún.* Lagos: Longman.

Olatunji (1982), *Adebayo Fálétí, Adebayo Fálétí, A Study of His Poem.* Ibadan: Heinemann Educational Books.

Ọlatunji (1982) *Ewì Adébáyọ̀ Fálétí, Ìwé kinni.* Ibadan: Heinemann Educational Books (Nigeria) Plc.

Olatunji (1985), *Features of Yoruba Oral Poetry.* Ibadan: University Press Plc.

Olukoju, E. (1994), *The Study of Yoruba Songs.* Ibadan: External Studies Programme.

Sotunsa Mobolanle, E. (2005), Features of Talking Drum Poetry, a Ph.D Thesis submitted to the Department of English, University of Ibadan, Ibadan, Nigeria.

Yemitan, O. (1963), *Ìjálá Aré Ọdẹ.* Ibadan: UPL.

Yemitan, O. (1970), *Ojú Òṣùpá, Apá kìíní.* Ibadan: Oxford University Press.

YOUR KNOWLEDGE HAS VALUE

- We will publish your bachelor's and
  master's thesis, essays and papers

- Your own eBook and book -
  sold worldwide in all relevant shops

- Earn money with each sale

Upload your text at www.GRIN.com
and publish for free